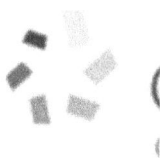

Drama for Students, Volume 32

Project Editor: Sara Constantakis Rights Acquisition and Management: Lynn Vagg Composition: Evi Abou-El-Seoud Manufacturing: Rhonda Dover Imaging: John Watkins

Digital Content Production: Edna Shy © 2015 Gale, Cengage Learning WCN: 02-200-210

ALL RIGHTS RESERVED. No part of this work covered by the copyright herein may be reproduced, transmitted, stored, or used in any form or by any means graphic, electronic, or mechanical, including but not limited to photocopying, recording, scanning, digitizing, taping, Web distribution, information networks, or information storage and retrieval systems, except as permitted under Section 107 or 108 of the 1976 United States Copyright Act, without the prior written permission of the publisher.

Since this page cannot legibly accommodate all

copyright notices, the acknowledgments constitute an extension of the copyright notice.

For product information and technology assistance, contact us at
Gale Customer Support, 1-800-877-4253.
For permission to use material from this text or product,
submit all requests online at
www.cengage.com/permissions.
Further permissions questions can be emailed to
permissionrequest@cengage.com While every effort has been made to ensure the reliability of the information presented in this publication, Gale, a part of Cengage Learning, does not guarantee the accuracy of the data contained herein. Gale accepts no payment for listing; and inclusion in the publication of any organization, agency, institution, publication, service, or individual does not imply endorsement of the editors or publisher. Errors brought to the attention of the publisher and verified to the satisfaction of the publisher will be corrected in future editions.

Gale
27500 Drake Rd.
Farmington Hills, MI, 48331-3535

ISBN-13: 978-0-7876-9642-9

ISSN 1094-9232

This title is also available as an e-book.
ISBN-13: 978-1-4103-9244-2
ISBN-10: 1-4103-9244-2
Contact your Gale, a part of Cengage Learning sales

representative for ordering information.

Printed in Mexico
1 2 3 4 5 6 7 19 18 17 16 15

Sweeney Todd: The Demon Barber of Fleet Street

Stephen Sondheim 2007

Introduction

The legend of Sweeney Todd, the demon barber, has been whispered throughout London for generations. Todd's entire life history can be recounted with remarkable detail: He was orphaned young and worked as a barber's apprentice until he was sentenced to five years in Newgate Prison for petty larceny. Upon his release, Todd set up shop on

Fleet Street, where he would slash the throats of his customers, then send the bodies to his neighbor, Mrs. Lovett, who used the victims' flesh to make meat pies. Todd stood trial, they say, and boasted of his many crimes. Mrs. Lovett, however, never made it to trial. After barely surviving the anger of a vengeful mob on her trip to prison, she poisoned herself in her cell.

In his book *The Wonderful and Surprising History of Sweeney Todd*, Robert L. Mack describes the many permutations of the story: the records of Todd's confessions in court, the old stories of people who remember the location of Mrs. Lovett's pie shop and others who have explored the labyrinth of secret passages under St. Dunstan's church on Fleet Street. It is "all very grimly fascinating, to be sure." writes Mack, "but not a word of it is true." The story of Sweeney Todd is but an urban legend, albeit one with a long history—like a ghost story told to thrill and frighten. In 1979, the legend was adapted into a successful Broadway show. Stephen Sondheim wrote the music and lyrics, and Hugh Wheeler wrote the book. Tim Burton's 2007 film version of this play is the most recent incarnation of Todd's story, adding another facet to the tale's theme of revenge and giving it a macabre humor. The film is rated R for its bloody violence and therefore is more suitable for older students.

Plot Summary

Anthony and the title character of *Sweeney Todd* arrive in London on a ship. Young Anthony anticipates the wonders of London, but Sweeney sees only the city's dark side. Sweeney hints to Anthony of his past: as he tells his story, the audience sees a sunlit flashback showing a young, smiling man with his beautiful wife and daughter, strolling through a flower market. An older man sees the happy family, fancies the woman, and has her husband taken away by the police.

After parting from Anthony, Sweeney goes to Mrs. Lovett's pie shop. She offers him one of her meat pies while admitting that her wares are completely unappetizing. Mrs. Lovett recognizes Sweeney as Benjamin Barker, who used to live with his family in the room upstairs from her shop. She explains what happened to his wife and daughter after he was transported to Australia for his supposed crimes: Lucy was tricked and attacked by Judge Turpin, who had Sweeney sent away. She was driven by the trauma to poison herself, and the judge took the infant daughter as his ward.

Mrs. Lovett takes Sweeney upstairs to his old room, which still holds some of his family's things, and retrieves his set of razors from their hiding place under the floorboards. Sweeney rejoices at having his razors again and readies himself for revenge.

While walking through the streets of London, Anthony sees a beautiful young woman in the window of a large house. It is love at first sight. A beggar woman approaches and tells Anthony that the girl's name is Johanna. Johanna is Judge Turpin's ward, and he keeps her strictly isolated. The judge sees Anthony and invites him inside the house. At first the judge pretends to be friendly, but soon he threatens Anthony for daring to look at Johanna. The judge has the beadle throw Anthony roughly out into the alley. Anthony vows to rescue Johanna from her cruel guardian.

FILM TECHNIQUE

- There are many scenes where Burton captures Sweeney's face in reflections. When Mrs. Lovett gives the razors back to Sweeney, he opens one, and the camera sees his reflection in the blade. After Sweeney sings "My Friends," he holds the razor up to the sunlight and says, "At last my arm is complete again." It is as if the razor gives him back a shred of his true identity. Reflections also capture Sweeney's mental state. For example, when Sweeney is upset that the beadle has not come yet, though he promised to show up within the week, Mrs. Lovett sings,

"Easy now. Hush, love, hush." However, her words cannot calm Sweeney. Sweeney's reflection is seen in a shattered mirror, which represents his frustration and anger. The broken mirror shows that his world and his identity are in pieces when he cannot pursue his one goal: revenge. A reflected image is also tied to identity when Sweeney sings, "my Lucy lies in ashes / And I'll never see my girl again, but the work waits, I'm alive at last." His reflection is seen in a puddle in the street, but in his despair he falls to his knees, and his hand, still holding a razor, splashes into the water, disturbing the surface and obscuring his reflection, as if he is losing his identity.

- Burton has a very distinctive directing approach—a recognizable mood and artistic style—but he was restrained in his adaptation of *Sweeney Todd*. Ryan Gilbey of *New Statesman* points out that some film versions of Broadway shows have increased the artificiality of the musical genre rather than simply portraying the story and allowing the viewer to enjoy the performances. Gilbey explains: "The trend in modern assaults on the genre [musical], as in *Chicago* or *Moulin Rouge*, has been towards chopping up the shots to achieve a berserk energy." Burton does not do this in *Sweeney Todd*. If anything, Burton uses more realistic, rather than stylistic, images. It is not like a play, where the camera remains at one angle, showing the entire scene as if the actors are on a stage. Sometimes the camera comes close to focus on the characters' expressions, and sometimes it shows the entire room to capture the mood of the setting and the movements of the actors' bodies. The choice of a close-up or a more distant shot seems to be naturally made, not drawing attention to itself. Gilbey praises Burton's directorial decisions, writing, "it's an exotic joy to be able to savour the scene without constant directorial interference."

- Johanna is almost a prisoner of the oily Judge Turpin, and Burton depicts her imprisonment by framing her with structures in the set. Anthony first sees her sitting in her bedroom window, where her captivity is also reinforced by the caged bird that sits next to her. The judge watches her through a peephole, and when she is forced into Mr. Fogg's asylum, again Anthony catches sight of her through a window, this time also captured by bars. Even when Johanna is not set into an obvious structural frame, she is always shown indoors. When Judge Turpin sends her away, she is immediately shoved into a carriage. Even when she escapes with Anthony, she is not shown running through the London streets—she appears in Sweeney's room. Her implied flight with Anthony is the only bit of hope at the end of the movie, but again Burton does not show it. Instead, the audience sees Sweeney threatening her with his razor and dashing off, leaving her terrified in his barber's chair.

Sweeney and Mrs. Lovett visit St. Dunstan's market. From a stage-like cart, a young boy named Toby sings to the crowd about "Pirelli's Miracle Elixir." Sweeney and Mrs. Lovett mumble in the background about how terrible the concoction smells. Pirelli appears, angered by someone speaking ill of his product.

Sweeney proposes a contest with Pirelli to determine who can give the closest shave most quickly. Pirelli agrees. He poses and draws out the drama of the contest, playing to the crowd, while Sweeney works efficiently, simply getting the job done. The beadle declares Sweeney the winner. Pirelli, angry at losing, gives Toby a slap and pushes him behind the curtain. The beadle promises to come to Sweeney's shop in Fleet Street within the week.

Johanna again sits in her window. The judge watches her through a peephole in the wall. Johanna opens the window to throw a key out to Anthony, who waits below.

Sweeney waits in his room, frustrated that the beadle has not come as promised. Mrs. Lovett tries to calm him. Anthony bursts in to ask for Sweeney's help in rescuing Johanna. Mrs. Lovett and Sweeney realize that Johanna is his lost daughter. Sweeney agrees to help.

Pirelli comes to speak with Sweeney. Mrs. Lovett keeps Toby downstairs, distracting him with meat pies. Pirelli reveals his true identity to Sweeney: he is really Daniel Higgins, who worked for Benjamin Barker as a boy. He recognizes the distinctive razors. Pirelli threatens to reveal Sweeney's past unless he receives half of Sweeney's earnings. In a panicked rage, Sweeney bashes Pirelli's head with the tea kettle, knocking him to the floor.

Toby realizes that Pirelli is in danger of being late for an appointment and rushes upstairs. Sweeney has hidden Pirelli in a large chest, but his fingers, barely moving, dangle out from under the lid. Sweeney gets rid of Toby by telling him to ask Mrs. Lovett for some gin. Sweeney finishes Pirelli off by slitting his throat.

Judge Turpin convicts a little boy for stealing and sentences him to death. As he leaves the court, the judge tells the beadle that he intends to marry Johanna, though she resists the idea. The beadle suggests a shave and leads him toward Sweeney's shop.

Mrs. Lovett leaves Toby with the bottle of gin and goes upstairs. She learns that Sweeney killed Pirelli but is not very troubled by the knowledge. She takes Pirelli's purse.

The judge and beadle arrive, and Mrs. Lovett leaves. Sweeney settles the judge in the barber's chair and listens to him speak of his impending marriage. Sweeney is about to cut the judge's throat when Anthony bursts in, speaking of Johanna. The judge, furious that Anthony has communicated with Johanna and angry at Sweeney for seeming to be in league with him, storms out.

Sweeney is livid at losing his chance with the judge and sends Anthony away. Mrs. Lovett returns and tries to soothe him. Sweeney vows to have vengeance, turning his anger on everyone in the city. Mrs. Lovett again tries to distract Sweeney, giving him a glass of gin. Mrs. Lovett comes up with the idea of getting rid of Pirelli's body by using his flesh to make meat pies. The two of them decide to make it a general plan: they will improve Mrs. Lovett's business by killing off Sweeney's customers.

Judge Turpin catches Johanna packing for her flight with Anthony. The judge has the beadle take Johanna away in a carriage. Anthony sees her shoved into the carriage and chases after her.

Toby sings to draw in customers to a grand reopening of Mrs. Lovett's pie shop. Business is booming. The customers love the new pies. The beggar woman lingers around the shop, and Mrs. Lovett yells at Toby to throw her out.

Sweeney rebuilds his barber's chair, adding gears and hinges, and cuts a trapdoor in the floor so that he can dump his victims down to the bakehouse to be turned into pies. A montage shows Sweeney thinking of Johanna as he kills customer after customer, while Anthony searches throughout the city for Johanna. The beggar woman sees the black smoke from the bakehouse and points out the terrible smells.

Mrs. Lovett, Sweeney, and Toby are having a picnic. Sweeney broods as Mrs. Lovett tells him about her dream of living with him by the sea. As she sings, the film shows a colorful fantasy sequence of their idyllic life and seaside wedding.

Sweeney still waits for his chance at revenge. Mrs. Lovett challenges him, asking if he can even remember what Lucy looked like. She suggests that she and Sweeney could build a life together. Anthony appears. He has found Johanna, locked in a madhouse. Sweeney proposes a plan in which Anthony would pretend to be an apprentice wig maker to gain entrance to the asylum, rescue Johanna, and bring her to Sweeney's room. Sweeney plans to lure the judge there by telling him of Anthony and Johanna's flight.

Sweeney gives Toby a message to take to the judge. Toby begins to suspect that Sweeney is a dangerous man and worries for Mrs. Lovett's safety. He promises to take care of her, and she realizes his suspicions. She leads him into the bakehouse under the pretense of showing him how to make the pies. She locks Toby in the bakehouse to protect Sweeney from any possible accusations.

Anthony manages to get into the asylum under his guise of apprentice wig maker. Mr. Fogg, who runs the asylum, leads him into the cell where Johanna is held. Anthony pulls a gun on Fogg, takes Johanna, and leaves Fogg at the mercy of the inmates.

Beadle Bamford comes to Mrs. Lovett's shop to investigate complaints of bad smells coming from her chimney. Sweeney distracts him, luring him upstairs with promises of a cologne that will please the ladies.

Toby, down in the bakehouse, helps himself to a meat pie. He finds a finger inside and then notices other human body parts around the room. He is frozen in horror until the body of the beadle falls down from Sweeney's trapdoor. Then Toby panics, banging on the locked door and shouting to Mrs. Lovett to let him out.

Anthony brings Johanna, disguised as a boy, to

Sweeney's room. He leaves her there, promising to return as soon as he can arrange for a coach to take them away. As Johanna waits, the beggar woman appears, looking for the beadle, and Johanna hides in the large chest.

After looking in vain for Toby in the sewer tunnels with Mrs. Lovett, Sweeney returns to his room. He tries to send the beggar woman away, but she does not go. He slashes her throat and sends her through the trapdoor to get rid of her before the judge arrives.

Sweeney tells the judge that Johanna is there and now eager to marry him. He convinces the judge to take a moment to primp, and once Sweeney has him in the chair, he reveals his true identity. The judge is terrified. Sweeney kills him, stabbing into his throat rather than slashing. The judge's blood sprays all over Sweeney.

Sweeney notices Johanna, watching from the chest. He pulls her out and shoves her into the chair, threatening her, but before he can do anything else, they hear a scream from downstairs. Sweeney rushes away after one last gesture with his razor and a warning that she should forget what she has seen.

Mrs. Lovett screams at the judge, telling him to die as he clutches her skirts. Sweeney appears just after the judge finally passes away. Mrs. Lovett tries to prevent Sweeney from seeing the beggar woman closely, but he finally recognizes her as his Lucy. He is furious with Mrs. Lovett, who claims she only let him think Lucy was dead to protect him. After a final grim waltz, Sweeney throws Mrs. Lovett into the fiery oven and slams the door. He goes to Lucy's body and cradles her in his arms. As he kneels on the floor, mourning, Toby creeps up through the sewer grate, takes up the fallen razor, and slits Sweeney's throat.

Characters

Beadle Bamford

Beadle Bamford (Timothy Spall) is Judge Turpin's right-hand man. He does the judge's dirty work, from kicking Anthony out into the street after the judge found him watching Johanna through her window to shoving Johanna into a carriage and hiding her away in Mr. Fogg's asylum. The beadle thinks well of himself, so Sweeney is able to play on his vanity to lure him up into the barber's chair, where he meets his bloody end.

Benjamin Barker

See Sweeney Todd

Johanna Barker

Johanna is Sweeney's daughter, who was an infant when Sweeney was transported to Australia. After Lucy Barker poisoned herself, Judge Turpin took Johanna as his ward. She lives in the judge's house like a prisoner. As the film begins, the judge decides he wants to take Johanna as his wife, but she has made a connection with young Anthony, who eventually helps her escape.

Lucy Barker

Lucy Barker is Sweeney's wife. The flashback shows the two of them happy together and besotted with their small daughter. Lucy's beauty attracts the attention of the unscrupulous Judge Turpin, who falsely convicts Sweeney (then called Benjamin Barker) and sends him to Australia to get rid of him. When Lucy still resists the judge's advances, he lures her to his house and attacks her. The trauma of the event pushes Lucy to attempt suicide. Many believe her dead, but the end of the story reveals that she was driven mad by the judge's cruel treatment of her. She now lives as a beggar woman in the streets, one of the few to see the black smoke over Mrs. Lovett's shop and recognize that something evil is going on.

Beggar Woman

See Lucy Barker

Mr. Fogg

Mr. Fogg runs the asylum where Judge Turpin sends Johanna so that she will learn to "appreciate what [she] has" and "think on [her] sins." Fogg calls the women in the asylum his "children," but he must not treat them kindly, because when Anthony rescues Johanna and leaves Fogg in the cell with the inmates, they seem ready to tear him limb from limb.

Daniel Higgins

See Adolfo Pirelli

Anthony Hope

Although Anthony has a relatively small amount of time on-screen, he is important in terms of plot and theme. Anthony's actions drive the subplot with Johanna and the judge, his intention to run away with Johanna inflaming the judge's jealousy. Anthony also serves as a foil for Sweeney throughout the film. In the very first scene, Anthony and Sweeney sing "there's no place like London." Innocent young Anthony says it in wonder, as if excited about the possibilities the city has to offer. Sweeney, however, thinks of London as "a great black pit" filled with the "vermin of the world." Sweeney's end is sad and bloody, but Anthony's implied escape with Johanna offers a shred of hope at the close of the film.

Mrs. Lovett

Mrs. Lovett, played by Helena Bonham Carter, is Sweeney's partner in crime. She comes up with the idea of getting rid of Sweeney's victims by baking their flesh into her meat pies. She tries to help him from the moment he returns to Fleet Street. Mrs. Lovett has romantic feelings for Sweeney, but he seems unaware of how much she cares. Her unrequited love for Sweeney drives her to lie to him, letting him believe that his wife, Lucy, is dead. She has unrealistic hopes about her relationship with Sweeney, imagining an idyllic life by the sea, but in the end her devotion to Sweeney makes her cruel—she and Sweeney search through the tunnels for Toby once he learns the truth about the meat pies, clearly intending to silence him.

Adolfo Pirelli

Sacha Baron Cohen plays Pirelli to great comic effect. When the audience first sees Pirelli, he is a laughable fop, with his ridiculous hairdo and his extravagant clothes. Soon, however, Pirelli's true colors shine through. He is petty and cruel to Toby, his young helper. Pirelli's real name is Daniel Higgins. He was an assistant of sorts to Benjamin Barker, so he recognizes Sweeney and attempts to blackmail him: Sweeney must give Pirelli half of his earnings to ensure his silence about his true identity. When Pirelli threatens Sweeney, he becomes the razor's first victim.

Toby

Toby first appears as Pirelli's assistant, hawking his "Miracle Elixir." After Pirelli's disappearance, Toby quickly joins Mrs. Lovett's cobbled-together family with Sweeney, becoming quite devoted to her. When Toby learns the truth about the source of the meat for Mrs. Lovett's pies, he is horrified. He manages to escape from her and Sweeney, and it is Toby who picks up Sweeney's razor and slits his throat, putting an end to his string of murders.

Sweeney Todd

Sweeney Todd (Johnny Depp) is the alias of Benjamin Barker, a young barber who was wrongly convicted of a crime because Judge Turpin was taken by the beauty of Mrs. Barker. When Sweeney escapes this unfair punishment and returns to London, he is determined to take his revenge. He sets up shop in his old rooms on Fleet Street. Sweeney forms an odd relationship with Mrs. Lovett, his landlady and partner in crime. She clearly adores him, and though he takes some comfort in her company and finds her help convenient, he does not return her affection equally.

Sweeney's need for revenge blots out everything else in his mind. He devotes his energy to figuring out how to lure the judge to him rather than trying to free his young daughter, Johanna, from the judge's clutches. When Judge Turpin slips through Sweeney's fingers the first time he is in the barber's chair, Sweeney turns his rage on other innocent customers. As he slashes throat after throat and dumps the bodies below to be turned into meat pies, he turns into a monster. It is only when he realizes that in his murderous rage he unknowingly killed his beloved if insane wife, Lucy, that Sweeney feels regret and remorse.

Judge Turpin

In spite of Sweeney's killing spree, Judge Turpin (Alan Rickman) is the true villain of the story. It is Judge Turpin who coveted Sweeney's wife and convicted him on trumped-up charges in an attempt to gain Lucy for himself. He attacked Lucy, driving her to attempted suicide and madness. He keeps his ward, Johanna—Lucy and Sweeney's daughter—as a virtual prisoner and tries to force her into marrying him. His motives are completely selfish.

Themes

Revenge

The entire plot of the film is centered around Sweeney Todd's quest for revenge. The opening scene shows Sweeney's return to London. He has come back to find his wife and daughter and to exact revenge on Judge Turpin, the man who falsely accused and convicted him of a crime and had him transported to Australia. The other elements of the story—Mrs. Lovett's pies and Anthony's rescue of Johanna—are all secondary plot lines that branch off from this main theme.

When Mrs. Lovett first comes up with the idea of hiding Pirelli's body by using his flesh for her meat pies, it is presented almost humorously. It is a ridiculous notion, and the song in which she and Sweeney discuss the possibility of continuing the scheme by killing others is comic. Because of the humor in the scene, the viewer does not balk at the idea, which is really quite horrific. Mrs. Lovett and Sweeney are thinking of their potential victims as meat, as a means to an end. She intends to use the innocent customers to make money, while Sweeney seems content to practice wielding his razor until he can reach the judge. The fact that they can think of murder so lightly shows how the need for revenge changes a person, taking away their humanity.

Sweeney's loss of humanity is also illustrated

by his thoughts about his daughter, which stand in stark contrast to Anthony's role in the plot. Anthony sees Johanna, and it is love at first sight. He wants to rescue her. His impulse is naïve and perhaps partially selfish, but he truly wants to help the girl. Sweeney, however, seems to have lost sight of what is best for his daughter. He thinks not of protecting her but only of punishing the judge.

The film shows that revenge consumes the person seeking it as much as the one who is to be punished. Sweeney loses himself and becomes a monster because of his drive for vengeance. In the climactic scenes, he lashes out at the beggar woman with his razor, killing her without thought. Murder has become almost a reflex for him. He unknowingly kills his beloved Lucy, and it is only when he realizes who she is that he understands how far he has fallen.

Family

The theme of family is strong in Sweeney Todd, but what is often a positive theme in film and literature has been twisted into something dark. Sweeney's family has been taken from him, and he believes his wife dead and his daughter lost to him. His loving feelings as a husband and father turn into a passion for revenge against Judge Turpin, the man responsible for his losses. It is soon after Sweeney seems to accept that he will not be able to get Johanna back from the judge, singing, "I'll never see my girl again," that he starts to exact his bloody vengeance on his unsuspecting customers.

In addition to the Barker family, there are examples of adoptive families, but they are no more successful. After Lucy Barker's death, Judge Turpin takes Johanna as his ward, but rather than caring for young Johanna and protecting her as a father should, the judge preys upon her. He keeps her captive in his house, watches her through a peephole, tries to force her to marry him, and even goes so far as to send her to a mental asylum to bend her to his will.

Mrs. Lovett tries to create another adoptive family with Sweeney and Toby, even if Sweeney is oblivious to her efforts. In the end, this family also fails: her desire for Sweeney is stronger than her maternal feelings for Toby, so when the boy discovers the truth about the murders, she goes after him with Sweeney, searching through the underground passages. The family unit is also disrupted because of the lie Mrs. Lovett lets Sweeney believe about Lucy's attempted suicide. When Sweeney discovers that Lucy survived the poison, he can no longer trust Mrs. Lovett and is furious with her.

READ. WATCH. WRITE.

- Famed film critic Roger Ebert writes of *Sweeney Todd*, "Burton fashions his musical in what can almost be described as an intimate style." Rather than showing "platoons of dancers in London squares," Burton cut out the large ensemble numbers included in the original stage productions of the show. Ebert approves this choice, pointing out that many of the songs are "confessional" and "anguished." Burton's directorial decisions indeed reinforce a close study of the characters. Rather than the big, broad view of a large stage production, the movie allows viewers to see the actors' expressions, as if standing nearby. How do the broader and the more intimate shots reflect what is going on in the story or what is happening in the characters' minds? Watch *Sweeney Todd* again, paying careful attention to where the director uses close-ups and where he uses wider shots. Write an essay explaining how Burton uses this basic element of film to enrich the story.

- Using print and online sources, research the urban legend of Sweeney Todd. What elements of the legend appear in Sondheim's play and Burton's film? Create a Power-Point presentation explaining the origin of the story and its various versions, and share the presentation with your class.

- Terry Hughes directed the 1982 movie version of *Sweeney Todd*, starring Angela Lansbury as Mrs. Lovett and George Hearn as Sweeney. Because Hughes filmed a stage production, watching the movie feels a lot like watching a Broadway show. Compare Hughes's and Burton's films. Do you think Burton was right to cut out some of the songs? Does it make the story seem more realistic? Or do you feel something is lost by cutting out ensemble numbers? Write an essay explaining your view.

- Watch Tom Hooper's 2012 film adaptation of the popular Broadway show *Les Mise´rables*. Unlike Sweeney Todd, Jean Valjean, the protagonist of *Les Mise´rables*, does commit a crime, but his sentence is far out of proportion to the severity of his crime. Rather than allowing the unfair conviction to twist his humanity and drive him to seek revenge, Valjean vows to escape from his past and remain a good man. Also, where Sweeney loses sight of his daughter's welfare, Valjean adopts a young girl and cares for her tenderly. While watching *Les Mise´rables*, think about how Valjean's reaction to his experience differs from Sweeney's. Write a short story in which Valjean and Sweeney meet and explain their attitudes: Sweeney's determination to rid the world of a wicked man and Valjean's decision to forgive and forget the past.

- Whether critics adore or loathe Burton's directorial style, they agree that his films have an undeniable visual impact. Watch Burton's *Charlie and the Chocolate Factory* (2005), which is based on Roald Dahl's classic novel and which also stars Johnny Depp. Just as *Sweeney Todd* has a specific visual style, with its gloomy rooms and dark, tattered costumes, the candy-colored fantasyland in *Charlie and the Chocolate Factory* creates a distinct mood. Select a scene from each movie in which the visual elements enhance what is going on with the story or the characterization. Create a blog in which you explain your opinions about each scene, and invite your classmates to comment about these and other visually interesting scenes in both films.

The only hope at the end of the story is the escape of Anthony and Johanna, which is only hinted at and not portrayed. The viewer can at least dream that the two young lovers will find some happiness, perhaps marrying and starting a family of their own.

Color

The color palette is so muted throughout *Sweeney Todd* that it almost appears to be a black-and-white film. London is full of shadows, and even when sunlight appears, it is weak and dull. Many of the costumes are black and white and shades of gray. Where color appears, it is subdued: the faded yellow in the wallpaper of Sweeney's room or the pale blue of Sweeney's short jacket.

The lack of color in the opening scenes makes the first flashback very surprising. Sweeney is shown with his wife and infant daughter, smiling. His happiness is reflected in the scene around him. The sunlight casts a warm yellow glow over everything. Instead of the grayish, sickly pallor that has been seen until that point, the characters' flesh shows color and life. They are surrounded by bright flowers.

In addition to the flashbacks, vibrant color appears in Mrs. Lovett's fantasy about living by the sea with Sweeney and Toby. The sky is blue, and Mrs. Lovett's gowns are cheerful pinks and reds. The color in the fantasy sequence sets it apart from the main narrative of the film, much like the flashbacks. It also shows Mrs. Lovett's unrealistic ideas about her relationship with Sweeney: although she smiles and wears vivid colors, his face is expressionless, and he is still dressed in black and white.

Then, as Sweeney's murderous rage swerves more and more out of control, Burton also introduces a lot of blood. The spurting red blood is all the more shocking when splashed across the grim, almost colorless scenes, the sleeves of Sweeney's white shirt, and his pale face. In one scene, Sweeney touches the black-and-white photograph of his wife and daughter with his bloody fingers, smearing the picture with red. Color illustrates to the viewer the terrible extent of his transformation from warm, smiling family man to cold, vengeful killer.

Blood and Violence

Sweeney Todd is rated R for "graphic bloody violence." It is indeed a bloody film, from the moment when Sweeney first slits Pirelli's throat to keep his identity a secret. In some ways, the blood is not all that alarming at first. Sweeney hitting Pirelli over the head with a teapot appears more disturbingly violent than when he actually kills him with the razor a few moments later. Because of the panic driving Sweeney to hit Pirelli with the kettle, that part of the scene has a desperation and an urgency to it that the later murders lack. Sweeney is usually in control during the killings that follow, calmly gliding his razor over his customers' throats.

Burton does not at first depict the bloody violence realistically. Peter Travers of *Rolling Stone* writes in a review of the film that "Burton's use of blood is impressionistic, not realistic." The blood spurts, splashes, and drips. The viewer gets the idea of a bloody horror film, but the lack of realism and the beautiful melodies subtract from the shock and horror the viewer might feel if the deaths were not portrayed with such over-the-top theatrics. Burton even introduces a very grim humor in the contrast between Sweeney's collected exterior and his brutal acts: his mind is clearly on other things as he kills customer after customer, singing of his missing daughter, "My little dove, my sweet." The juxtaposition of the tender endearments and the atrocious acts is both terrible and laughable.

Before too long, however, the cartoonish bloody violence gives way to the realism of grisly death. As A. O. Scott explains in a *New York Times* review,

> The initial geyser of blood may seem artificially bright, but when the bodies slide head first from the chair down a chute into the cellar, they crash and crumple with sickening literalness. You are watching human beings turned into meat.

Rather than the physical violence, it is Sweeney losing his humanity that is truly the most frightening thing about the film, and the viewer is brought along for the ride. Because the lack of realism encourages the audience not to think too closely about what Sweeney is doing, at some point during the film viewers realize that they too have been thinking of his victims as expendable, as somehow less than human, or, like Mrs. Lovett, as "fresh supplies."

The Bloody Code

England's penal system throughout the eighteenth and nineteenth centuries is known as the Bloody Code. It is so called because there were so many comparatively minor crimes that could be punished by the death penalty. For example, the theft of anything worth over five shillings (about fifty US dollars in today's money) could receive the death penalty. There was no mercy: in *Sweeney Todd*, Judge Turpin is shown condemning a little boy to death for stealing. The goal was to punish rather than to rehabilitate.

The number of crimes that could result in the death penalty in England increased hugely during the eighteenth century: in 1688, there were fifty crimes punishable by death, but by 1815, there were over two hundred. The penal code was stern for many reasons. First, the laws were created by wealthy men, many of whom were very unsympathetic. They believed that people committed crimes because they were lazy or greedy, not understanding that genuine, desperate poverty might drive someone to steal. Also, the wealthy lawmakers wanted to protect what was theirs and therefore made laws to maintain the social order that kept the poor in their place.

The severe penalties were meant to prevent

people from committing crimes. For the same reason, executions were public. The disproportionate sentences were intended to scare citizens into behaving. In practice, however, the severe sentencing sometimes had the reverse effect: because criminals knew they would be killed for theft even if they spared their victims, they might resort to murder to leave no witnesses.

Transportation

An alternative to the death penalty was transportation, which is what happened to Sweeney when Judge Turpin wrongly convicted him. In 1788, the first group of prison ships, called the First Fleet, arrived in Botany Bay in the Australian colony of New South Wales, bringing almost eight hundred British convicts, as well as a troop of British marines and their families. During the end of the eighteenth century and the first half of the nineteenth century, approximately 160,000 convicts were sent to Australia. The prisoners were mostly poor and illiterate. Most were convicted for larceny (theft of personal property).

When they arrived in the colony, the convicts were put to work. If they had experience in a useful trade, such as carpentry or farming, they would work in that capacity. If the prisoners could read and write, they might work for the governors of the colony, keeping records and maintaining correspondence.

Convicts might be released early for good

behavior, which could significantly reduce the length of their sentences. For example, a seven-year sentence might be reduced to only four years. Some were even granted full pardons for their crimes. Although the paroled convicts were not usually allowed to return home, many were granted land to settle. This was a way for the British Empire to expand its Australian colony. The practice of transportation in England lasted until 1853. It ended because many believed transportation was too harsh a sentence and because the Australian colonies were thriving and no longer required the added population.

Critical Overview

Critical reception of Burton's *Sweeney Todd* was overwhelmingly positive. When rumors of the production began to circulate, there were certainly doubts about its success. In *The Wonderful and Surprising History of Sweeney Todd*, Robert L. Mack explains that "the news that Burton would once again be teaming up with Depp … was initially greeted with dismay by some Sondheim devotees." Neither Depp nor Carter had ever sung on-screen before, much less with such challenging compositions. Lisa Schwarzbaum, in an *Entertainment Weekly* review, calls the project "an impossible assignment," but one that Burton managed "with more-than-respectable panache." Sondheim himself seemed pleased with the results. Mack quotes Sondheim from during production:

> Sometimes a story or stage production has to wait a long time until the right people come together to turn it into a motion picture.… That's what has happened with *Sweeney Todd*, and I'm excited as well as confident that it will be a first-rate and startling movie.

Ryan Gilbey of *New Statesman* writes that "Burton's freak-show sensibility" is a perfect fit for the dark themes of the story. Writing for the *New York Times*, A. O. Scott describes *Sweeney Todd* as "something close to a masterpiece," and Peter Travers of *Rolling Stone* writes, "*Sweeney Todd* is a thriller-diller from start to finish: scary, monstrously funny and melodically thrilling." Travers names Burton "a true visionary, and with the help of cinematographer Dariusz Wolski, costume whiz Colleen Atwood and production designer Dante Ferretti he sets a new gold standard for bringing a stage musical to the screen."

Several critics draw particular attention to the look of the film. Roger Ebert praises the "brooding production design," calling the movie "a feast for the eyes and the imagination." Travers describes the film as "a spellbinder of breathtaking beauty and terror" that is "brilliantly conceived and executed." In 2008, Dante Ferretti and Francesca Lo Schiavo won the Academy Award for Best Production Design for the film.

The actors in the major roles also receive much admiration from critics. Gilbey calls Depp's and Carter's performances "enchanting." Ebert describes the work of Depp, Carter, and Rickman as "merciless" in its emotional depth. Depp in particular draws glowing reviews. Travers writes that "Depp is simply stupendous," blurring "the line between acting and singing, fusing them into something that keeps the movie blazing." Burton and Depp's long working relationship tells in the quality of the production, as Ebert describes Depp as "a perfect instrument" for Burton's vision.

What Do I See Next?

- *Little Shop of Horrors* (1986), directed by Frank Oz and starring Rick Moranis, Ellen Greene, and Steve Martin, is an adaptation of a Broadway musical. The film, rated PG-13, tells the story of Seymour Kreborn, who is driven to murder to protect the girl he loves and to feed the appetites of a supernatural, bloodthirsty plant.

- Burton and Depp first worked together on *Edward Scissorhands* (1990). Tim Burton wrote and directed the film, which is rated PG-13 and stars Depp and Winona Ryder. The story is an odd, modern fairy tale of sorts that shows many of the stylistic elements for which

Burton has become well known. Edward is the product of a reclusive inventor, who died before he could finish his creation. Therefore, Edward has scissors in place of hands. Though he is a gentle soul, he cannot always control the sharp blades.

- In Frank Capra's *Arsenic and Old Lace* (1944, unrated), Cary Grant stars as a newly married man who visits his elderly maiden aunts to tell them the news of his wedding. During his visit, he learns that the two ladies have been poisoning lonely old men and burying them in the cellar. The murders are pity killings rather than products of revenge, but the movie has a black humor similar to that in *Sweeney Todd*.

- Alexandre Dumas's novel *The Count of Monte Cristo* (1844–1845), a classic story of revenge, has been adapted into films several times over the years. The 2002 version, directed by Kevin Reynolds and rated PG-13, makes some changes to the plot and characters but adds a lot of fun and action to the well-known story.

- Rob Reiner portrays a lighter take on the theme of revenge in *The*

Princess Bride (1987), which stars Cary Elwes, Mandy Patinkin, and Robin Wright. It is based on the 1973 novel by William Goldman. This film is rated PG.

- William Shakespeare's play *Titus Andronicus* was adapted into *Titus* (1999) by Julie Taymor, who both directed and wrote the screenplay. Anthony Hopkins fills the title role brilliantly. The R-rated film is a disturbing and bloody exploration of the theme of revenge.

Sources

"Australian History: Convicts," Australian History, http://www.australianhistory.org/convicts (accessed August 13, 2014).

"Convicts and the British Colonies in Australia," Australian Government website, http://australia.gov.au/about-australia/australian-story/convicts-and-the-britishcolonies (accessed August 13, 2014).

Ebert, Roger, Review of *Sweeney Todd: The Demon Barber of Fleet Street*, RogerEbert.com, December 20, 2007, http://www.rogerebert.com/reviews/sweeney-todd-the-demonbarber-of-fleet-street-2007 (accessed August 7, 2014).

Gilbey, Ryan, "Sing for Your Supper," in *New Statesman*, January 2008, p. 43.

Gribben, Mark, "Sweeney Todd," in *Crime Library: Criminal Minds & Methods*, http://www.crimelibrary.com/serial_killers/weird/too (accessed August 12, 2014).

Logan, John, *Sweeney Todd: The Demon Barber of Fleet Street* (script), IMSDb, http://www.imsdb.com/Movie Scripts/Sweeney Todd: The Demon Barber of Fleet Street Script.html (accessed August 12, 2014).

Mack, Robert L., "Maybe It's Because I'm a Londoner: True Lies and the Life of an Urban

Legend," in *The Wonderful and Surprising History of Sweeney Todd: The Life and Times of an Urban Legend*, Continuum, 2007, pp. 71–97.

———, "Swing Your Razor Wide, Sweeney: Further Adventures of a Legend," in *The Wonderful and Surprising History of Sweeney Todd: The Life and Times of an Urban Legend*, Continuum, 2007, pp. 303–304.

"Prison and Penal Reform in the 1800s," My Learning, http://www.mylearning.org/prison-and-penal-reform-inthe-1800s/p-3270/ (accessed August 13, 2014).

Schwarzbaum, Lisa, Review of *Sweeney Todd: The Demon Barber of Fleet Street*, in *Entertainment Weekly*, December 12, 2007, http://www.ew.com/ew/article/0,,20165791,00.html (accessed August 7, 2014).

Scott, A. O., "Murder Most Musical," in *New York Times*, December 21, 2007, http://www.nytimes.com/2007/12/21/movies/21swee_r=0 (accessed August 7, 2014).

Sweeney Todd: The Demon Barber of Fleet Street, directed by Tim Burton, Warner Bros., 2007, DVD.

Travers, Peter, Review of *Sweeney Todd: The Demon Barber of Fleet Street*, in *Rolling Stone*, December 13, 2007, http://www.rollingstone.com/movies/reviews/sweene todd-20071213 (accessed August 7, 2014).

Further Reading

Burton, Tim, *The Melancholy Death of Oyster Boy & Other Stories*, Rob Weisbach Books, 1997.

> In addition to his work in film, Burton is a published author and illustrator. This collection of darkly humorous stories reflects his interest in the outcasts and misfits of the world.

De Charmoy, Cozette, *True Life of Sweeney Todd: A Collage Novel*, Gaberbocchus Press, 1973.

> De Charmoy presents one telling of the urban legend of Sweeney Todd. Although this book is out of print, used paperback copies are not difficult to find online.

Vlastnik, Frank, and Ken Bloom, *Broadway Musicals: The 101 Greatest Shows of All Time*, Black Dog & Leventhal Publishers, 2004.

> Vlastnik and Bloom offer analyses of many enduring Broadway favorites. In addition to comprehensive background and detailed commentary, the volume includes production photographs, cast and song lists, and plot summaries.

Wood, Scott, *London Urban Legends: The Corpse on the Tube and Other Stories*, History Press, 2013.

The story of Sweeney Todd has been retold so often that many Londoners are convinced that he actually existed. Many of the city's other popular urban legends are explained or debunked by Wood in this entertaining volume.

Suggested Search Terms

Stephen Sondheim AND Sweeney Todd

Sweeney Todd AND urban legend

Tim Burton AND Sweeney Todd

Tim Burton AND directing style

Tim Burton AND Johnny Depp

Broadway AND Sweeney Todd

transportation to Australia

Bloody Code

Lightning Source UK Ltd.
Milton Keynes UK
UKHW020113080223
416599UK00009B/669

9 780270 528787